SOCIAL ANXIETY SOLUTIONS

CONQUER SOCIAL ANXIETY'S

By
VICTOR NWABUGO.C

TABLE OF CONTENT

TABLE OF CONTENTS

WHAT IS SOCIAL ANXIETY

A chronic mental health condition in which social interactions cause irrational anxiety.

For people with social anxiety disorder, everyday social interactions cause irrational anxiety, fear, self-consciousness and embarrassment

CHAPTER 1

EXERCISE REGULARLY:

If you work out consistently, a decent workout can reduce your stress and improve your ability to handle challenges. But can persons with severe anxiety benefit from exercise? Physical activity has been shown in studies to not only lessen anxiety symptoms but also enhance the quality of life.

Although the exact mechanism by which exercise reduces anxiety is unknown, experts think that several factors most likely play a role. One reason is those exercise increases endorphins, the body's feel-good hormone. By generating additional feel-good brain chemicals that affect neurotransmitters, exercise likely reduces anxiety. Additionally, it raises body temperature, which helps to promote calm. Exercise can increase confidence and self-esteem, and when done with others, it can promote social interaction.

Researchers who have studied the relationship between exercise and anxiety have advised practitioners to strongly advise patients with anxiety to engage in regular exercise in addition to following tried-and-true therapy regimens. Regular exercise has a wealth of advantages beyond improving mood, including lowering blood pressure, decreasing the risk of cancer and heart disease, and preventing diabetes.

The activity levels of their clients with anxiety are frequently checked by therapists who offer anxiety counseling. Nearly all forms of exercise can reduce anxiety, but studies suggest that some may be more anxiolytic than others.

In numerous circumstances, it has been demonstrated that yoga, in particular, helps people feel less stressed and anxious. A study conducted after the 2004 Andaman tsunami examined how yoga affected 47 survivors' levels of dread, anxiety, melancholy, and sleep issues. As indicators, measurements of skin resistance, respiration rate, and pulse rate were taken. All markers showed a significant decline, indicating that yoga was an effective strategy for managing anxiety and stress, especially when used in conjunction with treatment.

In other studies, yoga has been shown to lessen anxiety symptoms in persons with cancer, irritable bowel syndrome, eating disorders, and cardiovascular disease. Yoga can also be practiced by persons of any age and is simple to modify for those with disabilities.

Psychotherapy and medication are frequently used as treatments for anxiety disorders. Therapy frequently involves the therapist making an effort to increase the client's motivation for self-care activities including exercise, diet, and sleep.

When you hear the word "exercise," you might picture running laps around the block until you're exhausted. However, exercise encompasses a variety of activities that increase your level of activity and make you feel better. Running and weightlifting are both excellent cardiovascular exercises, but even brisk walking has health benefits. Many people claim that less strenuous hobbies like car washing, gardening, and other household chores can also assist to lower anxiety. any sort of physical activity that gets the body moving is likely to reduce anxiety and promote mental calmness.

Adults may discover that even modest quantities of exercise have an immediate impact on their anxiety symptoms.

And although practically any form of exercise can be beneficial for overall health, evidence indicates that these exercises, in particular, may reduce the symptoms of anxiety.

Cardio

You don't have to be an outstanding athlete to reap the rewards of physical activity for your mental health. According to research, any form of exercise that enhances your heart's and lungs' capacity to supply oxygen to your muscles as you work out will lessen anxiety. Additionally, there are several ways to exercise, including brisk walking, biking, swimming, and running.

One tiny study looked at how a single bout of aerobic exercise affected persons with various levels of anxiety, and it was published in the journal Cognitive Behaviour Therapy in 2015. Researchers divided participants into two groups at random: an aerobics group that exercised for 30 minutes; and a control group that stretched. They then examined the participants' levels of anxiety before, during, and after exercise, as well as three and seven days later. As expected, those who participated in aerobic exercise showed temporary decreases in anxiety sensitivity, but those in the control group did not.

Running can be beneficial as well/if that's your thing. Serotonin and norepinephrine, our bodies"feel good" neurotransmitters, are permanently altered by running, both during and after exercise. He stated that exercising can make it simpler for you to get to sleep at night. Your mood will improve, your stress levels will decrease, and your ability to think properly will all be enhanced by getting enough sleep.

Nature strolls

How about some help from Mother Nature to calm your nerves? Moving your body in natural environments may have therapeutic effects, at least temporarily, according to an emerging body of studies. "The presence of nature calms the mind," For instance, a 2015 study found that when young people went on a 50-minute nature walk, they felt less worried and had better memory performance. The study was published in the journal Landscape and Urban Planning.

CHAPTER 2

TEACH PROBLEM-SOLVING SKILLS:

Public speaking exercises
Finding opportunities to practice public speaking is a useful strategy for folks who have a mild-to-moderate social anxiety disorder, such as when it's not causing you panic episodes. joining a club like Toastmasters, which focuses on practicing and perfecting public speaking.

Consider CBT as a treatment option.
Among the several psychotherapies available, cognitive behavioral therapy is a useful method for treating social anxiety because it involves changing how you feel and think about a situation, which can then help you change your behavior. With social anxiety specifically, you want to identify thought patterns that make you avoid social situations, such as if a person is fixated on the possibility that someone will notice them blushing, sweating, or stammering. You want to help them learn to

challenge those expectations and adopt more positive self-talk rather than negative self-talk.

Slowly expose yourself to situations that make you anxious.
circumstance exposure Work up from simpler to more complex social situations while utilizing relaxation techniques to identify the social circumstances you are most uncomfortable in. Start by going out with a friend alone if you have a fear of large gatherings and have been staying away from group activities, she advises. Work your way up to going out with only a few pals, then. Before attempting to enter a restaurant, a bar, or a party where there would be more people, repeat as necessary until you feel more at ease. Together with a therapist, you can focus on situational exposure. Exposure therapy is a sort of treatment that a licensed psychologist can offer, just like cognitive behavioral therapy.

Ask for assistance from those who are there for you. Admitting to the people in your life that you experience social anxiety and may require assistance can be humiliating or humbling. However, it might be quite helpful to let a friend or family member know you might need some additional support. People will frequently feel better at ease if they are with a close friend or family member in a social setting. "Having a companion when you enter a social event for the first time might be useful, especially if someone has been very alone recently."

The key to providing support is encouraging an anxious individual to gradually gain more independence. People with more severe cases of social anxiety will eventually find it difficult to order food or go shopping alone. You should strike a balance between offering assistance and encouraging someone to do it themselves.

Bring them up in the conversation if you're a friend or family member of someone who struggles with social anxiety. "You would assume, 'Oh, Sara probably has something she would like to say about that. She's pretty curious about that," "You may help them by assisting them in emerging from their shells." However, make careful to first confirm with the person that doing so is acceptable. "If you have social anxiety, you might not like being forced to speak up in front of others. Beforehand, discuss with that person how they prefer to handle specific situations.

Be honest with yourself.
Even if you're the only one experiencing anxiety, it's simple to spiral while you're out in public and focuses on everything that seems to be going wrong. "In the now, you must put your attention elsewhere and tell yourself, "This is probably anxiousness. They can't read my thinking. I'm unsure of what they're thinking of me.

Of course, this is easier said than done, so she proposes employing a method called "five senses," which can assist you in regaining perspective and remaining present. "Check in with all five of your senses to help you become more aware of the outside world. Take your mind off uncomfortable internal feelings and bad thoughts. You can then attempt to refocus by asking yourself, "What are they saying to me? What else is happening at the moment? How do I see? What sound do I hear? What am I feeling?

Search for the bright side and practice self-kindness. It's quite natural if your social anxiety isn't dissipating as quickly as you'd want. It's possible that you moved too quickly and need to practice other social situations more before you're ready for the one you're stuck on, or that you need to practice relaxation and distraction tactics more so you can handle that circumstance the next time.

It might also be helpful to consider what caused a reaction, whether a panic attack or something else, after the fact. Try to deconstruct the question into, "How can I think about that differently?" or "How can I modify the scenario next time?" "Say you attend a concert and begin to experience a panic attack because you are surrounded by many people. If you feel nervous or confined, you can consider sitting near the back or on an aisle the next time, or choosing a spot where you can easily leave.

Most of the time, other individuals are much more preoccupied with themselves than with others. They are probably not observing how you act in social settings since they are preoccupied with deciding what to say or do next, the author claims. "Your anxiety typically highlights the negative and downplays the positive, so the aspects of yourself that you are keenly aware of may not stand out to others."

When to be concerned about anxiety's visible symptoms
Physical symptoms might also result from social anxiety disorders. Blushing, perspiration/ or a subjective feeling of being suddenly chilly or warm are all possible symptoms. Additionally, you might be physically tense, which could result in aches and sensations like a stomachache.

Even if you don't have a full-blown panic attack, you can still have signs of panic. According to, the symptoms of panic include a racing heart, shortness of breath, a sense of being out of control, or a fear of abrupt, imminent doom. Typically, those who have social anxiety will also experience some of these symptoms at a lower threshold.

It might be challenging to determine whether these symptoms are caused by anxiety or a more severe medical problem. "It's more probable what you are feeling is anxiety," "If the discomfort goes away fast after the anxiety-provoking circumstance has finished, and if you have a subjective sensation that you are currently terrified of anything." But if you're unsure, you should speak with a doctor about it to learn about specific symptoms to watch for and your risk factors.

This guidance is particularly more crucial if you have a known cardiac issue. She advises being extremely cautious when seeking medical attention for any of these kinds of symptoms. And you should discuss how to distinguish the two with your doctor if you have both cardiac issues and anxiety.

CHAPTER 3

SIT AND COMMUNICATE WITH THEM:

Having positive interactions with other people can help you live a life that is far less stressful and anxious. having more friends can serve as a "buffer" for anxious and depressed moods, therefore increasing your social support is associated with overall improved mental health. But for other people, social phobia and relationship-building are caused in part by anxiety, which makes them avoid social situations. This is particularly true if you suffer from social anxiety and are eager to make friends but are either too afraid to do so or are unaware of how to accomplish so.

The unfortunate side effect of avoiding social interactions is that you never get the chance to:

Boost your self-confidence in communication with others
Develop effective communication skills to boost your chances of forming lasting relationships.
For instance, if you are uncomfortable asking someone out on a date or attending parties, it will be significantly

harder for you to know how to handle these circumstances because of your inexperience and/or lack of confidence (like what to wear, what to say, etc.). People frequently possess the required abilities but lack the confidence to put them to use. In either case, practice will boost your self-assurance and enhance your communication abilities.

Why Is Communication a Vital Skill?

The secret to making (and maintaining) friends and creating a solid social support system is effective communication. They also assist you in meeting your wants while being considerate of those of others. Like any other talent, effective communication is something that must be mastered through repetition and error.

You may want to practice the following three communication skills:

communicating using body language
conversing abilities
Assertiveness

Of course, there are numerous facets to effective communication, so you might require more specialized assistance in some areas (e.g. learning how to deal with conflict, presentation skills, giving feedback, etc.). Please refer to the "Recommended Readings" section after this module for more detailed guidance.

Nonverbal Interaction

We communicate with one other largely through nonverbal means. Your body language and the way you look at other people can be just as influential as the words you use. You might act in ways meant to avoid social interaction when you're feeling worried. You might, for instance, speak softly or avoid making eye contact. In other words, you are attempting to remain silent to avoid being negatively seen by others. Your voice and body language do, however, send strong signals to people about you that include

condition of mind (e.g. impatience, fear)
Approach to the listener (e.g. submissiveness, contempt)
understanding the subject
(Do you have a hidden agenda?) Honesty
So, if you are speaking quietly, avoiding eye contact, and standing far away from other people, you are probably saying, "Stay away from me!" or "Don't talk to me!" Most likely, this is not the message you want to convey.

Having Conversations
A person with social anxiety may find it difficult to initiate and maintain discussions. Making small talk might be challenging because it's not always simple to come up with conversation starters. This is particularly valid when experiencing anxiety. On the other hand, some worried persons talk excessively, which may come across poorly to others.

Assertiveness

Honest expressing one's needs/wants, and feelings while respecting those of the other person constitutes assertive communication. Assertive communication is taking ownership of your activities while maintaining a non-threatening, non-judgmental demeanor.

You might find it challenging to speak openly about your ideas and feelings if you suffer from social anxiety. Learning assertiveness techniques can be challenging, especially given that being assertive may need you to hold back from acting in a way that is more natural for you. For instance, you might avoid expressing your thoughts, avoid provoking a debate, and constantly follow the crowd. You might have become inactive in your communication as a result. Alternately, you can have an aggressive communication style and strive to dominate and control others.

However, communicating assertively has a lot of advantages. For instance, you might be able to relate to people more openly and honestly while feeling less agitated and resentful. It also lessens emotions of helplessness and provides you with greater control over your life. It also gives OTHER individuals the freedom to live their own lives.

CHAPTER 4

START SMALL:

Do all you can at a time; dream big but start small. If you consume too much at once, you can vomit your dreams. Take each one one at a time and don't overindulge in your dreams! Dream big, but begin modestly.
It's okay, to begin with little adjustments while managing social anxiety. You're not required to approach everyone you meet and offer to lead a meeting.

Here are a few concepts to consider:

Avoid using the self-checkout at the store and try to strike up a conversation with the clerk instead.
To ask a question in class, raise your hand.
laud the attire of a student or coworker.
Invite a few close friends and family members over for a modest gathering; mingling in your home can make you feel more at ease.
Renaming anxious emotions can be helpful for some people.

Try thinking "I'm so excited to see what people are like outside of work!" instead of "I feel so scared about tonight."

CHAPTER 5

FOCUS MORE ON PRACTICING, PROGRESS, NOT PERFECTION:

Although it can result in self-defeating attitudes or habits that make it more difficult to accomplish goals, perfectionism is frequently considered a desirable attribute that boosts your chances of success. Stress, anxiety, sadness, and other mental health problems could potentially result from it. It may be beneficial for those who seek perfection out of emotions of inadequacy or failure to speak with a therapist; doing so can frequently help people control their excessive self-criticism.

List everything.

Make a list of your social objectives and rank them in order of least to most likely to cause anxiety.

Create plans.
Write down in detail the steps you will take to achieve each of these social goals.

To the point.
Think of a 0 to 10 anxiety scale with the following values: 0 represents complete calmness, 3 represents a low level of anxiety, 5 represents a moderate level of anxiety, 7 represents a high level of anxiety, and 10 represents panic. to better understand your anxiety and its patterns, rate your anxiety on a scale of one to ten.

Avoid using drinks or drugs to ease your anxiousness. Alcohol and drugs may give users a fleeting sense of false assurance.

Create and use soothing techniques.
encouraging self-coaching
focused inhalation
muscles are relaxed.
Distraction
Exercise

Match the soothing technique that best suits your level of anxiety.
If your anxiety level is a "3," some targeted breathing and constructive self-coaching can probably help you manage it successfully. Splashing cold water on your

face or performing some stretching exercises might be advised if your anxiety level is a "5". If your anxiety level is a "7," it could be useful to count backward from 100 by 7s (100, 93, 86, 79, 72, etc.) and practice belly breathing. You might wish to leave the location and take a walk if your anxiety is a "10." You see what I mean! It could take some trial and error to determine what works best for you.

Maintaining awareness of the present moment is mindfulness.
The past is over and the future is still in the future. Bring all of your attention to the current moment... do not criticize yourself.

Recognize and value incremental improvement.
Make a note of what worked throughout your social practice session and give yourself positive feedback. Your ANXIETY will make an effort to turn on your internal critic/but just ignore it. Remind yourself how brave it was for you to face your social anxiety, and how proud you should be of yourself. And with additional practice sessions, you'll keep advancing on your imperfect results. Step by step, please!

Be aware of how you present yourself verbally and nonverbally.
When speaking, project your voice, adjust the volume, and talk clearly. Put your shoulders back, head up, eyes open, and posture full when communicating nonverbally. Practice walking with pride and assurance. Get to know

your face and the way you appear to others while looking in a mirror. Practice laughing, letting go of worrying nonverbal body language, and smiling both with your mouth and your eyes. When you're uncomfortable, resist the urge to bury your face in your phone! This could give the wrong impression to people that you're preoccupied and they shouldn't bother you.

practice introducing yourself.
The Internet is full of fantastic resources that can be used for this. Practice introducing yourself, saying hello, asking a question, and making small talk with family members and close friends. Create specialized questions in advance that can be used with particular groups of people.

Continue to practice, practice, practice, and be pleased with yourself.

By

VICTOR NWABUGO.C

www.ingramcontent.com/pod-product-compliance
Lightning Source LLC
LaVergne TN
LVHW052115160826
845678LV00015B/3576

* 9 7 9 8 8 4 5 6 9 8 6 7 4 *